# A Gift

## called

# Gracy

## Lida Basson

Grosvenor House
Publishing Limited

This book is published by
Grosvenor House Publishing Ltd
Link House
140 The Broadway, Tolworth, Surrey, KT6 7HT.
www.grosvenorhousepublishing.co.uk

A CIP record for this book
is available from the British Library

Paperback ISBN 978-1-80381-770-5
Hardback ISBN 978-1-80381-771-2
eBook ISBN 978-1-80381-851-1

# Dedication

I dedicate this book to my beloved niece, Gabriella Basson, who is the apple of my eye. She has got the most beautiful heart and loves animals just as much as her auntie Lida. She's a precious daughter of our Lord Jesus and I know He is going to use her mightily for His Kingdom purposes.

Gabby, may you always know your true identity in Christ and walk in His power and authority to rule and reign with our King Jesus.

# Contents

# Introduction

The Lord asked me to write 'A Gift called Gracy' a year ago to share my faith journey during a 5-year season of my life that was marked by Jesus's grace, love and kindness.

A season where I got to know my King. Learning to trust Him every step of the way. Knowing that He is faithful and good and that He makes sure everything works out for my good, no matter how uncertain things may look at the time.

I pray that you will experience a touch of the Holy Spirit while reading this book that will make you hungry for more of Jesus to know Him on a personal level that will change your life forever.

# Chapter 1

# Stepping into a new season

*Yes, all things work for your enrichment so that more of God's marvellous grace will spread to more and more people, resulting in an even greater increase of praise to God, bringing him even more glory!*

2 Corinthians 4:15 TPT

It was end of February 2017 in the UK. The days were short, cold and dark... At the age of 42, I was at a place in my life that I never thought I would be. My heart felt empty and I was filled with disappointment. My marriage was over and all of a sudden all my dreams I had for the future had dissolved into nothing...

My husband and I had just separated and everything I had dreamt of and believed that my future would look like, was suddenly hanging in the air and looked very uncertain. We had recently moved to a new area in the English countryside where I didn't have any friends or family living close by. I was completely isolated and although I couldn't see the path ahead for myself, I knew one thing and one thing only... that the Lord was with me. He's my rock, He's faithful and He will help me and lead me through this wilderness. He will make a way where I couldn't see one at all. That was all I needed to know…

At this point, the Lord was leading me into a new season of my life. Although it was a very lonely and very challenging season, it was also a season of tremendous growth in my relationship with Him as He poured out His grace on me and led me through this 'wilderness'. Every step of the way He was right by my side, closer than my own breath.

*Where can I go from your Spirit?*
*Where can I flee from your presence?*
*If I go up to the heavens, you are there;*
*If I make my bed in the depths, you are there.*
*If I rise on the wings of the dawn,*
*If I settle on the far side of the sea,*
*even there Your hand will guide me,*
*Your right hand will hold me fast.*

Psalm 139:7-10 NIV

Although it was the hardest time of my life, I look back at it now and know that it truly is only in those seasons (if we will allow God), that He will come in and transform you into His best version of yourself, reflecting His true beauty and bringing you through and out of it stronger than ever before. Giving you the knowledge that you CAN do ALL things through Christ who strengthens you and that with God absolutely nothing is impossible.

> *My fellow believers, when it seems as though you are facing nothing but difficulties, see it as an invaluable opportunity to experience the greatest joy that you can!*
>
> *For you know that when your faith is tested, it stirs up power within you to endure all things. And then as your endurance grows even stronger it will release perfection into every part of your being until there is nothing missing and nothing lacking.*

James 1:2 TPT

Transformation isn't always easy. It's mostly uncomfortable and uncertain and all you can really do, is trust the Lord and as you trust Him more, your faith grows stronger and stronger deep inside of you. You step deeper and deeper into intimacy with Jesus as He develops your character.

> *Then, by constantly using your faith, the life of Christ will be released deep inside of you, and the resting place of His love will become the very source and root of your life.*

Ephesians 3:17 TPT

You need to get to a place where you are ready to completely die to yourself, your flesh, your own will and your emotions and surrender yourself completely to God, so that the Lord can come in and 'Resurrect' you into a completely New Creation in Him.

*For since we are permanently grafted into Him to experience a death like His, we are permanently grafted into Him to experience a resurrection like His and the New life that it imparts.*

Romans 6:5 TPT

*My old identity has been co-crucified with Messiah and no longer lives; for the nails of His cross crucified me with Him. And now the essence of this new life is no longer mine, for the Anointed One lives His life through me – we live in Union as one!*

Galatians 2:20 TPT

At one stage during the formation of a butterfly inside its cocoon, everything around it looks so dark and uncertain but through the growth of the butterfly, and the struggle to break out of that cocoon, the butterfly actually becomes stronger and stronger. Eventually, the cocoon breaks open and the beautiful butterfly flies out as a 'New Creation'. More beautiful than ever before and completely transformed.

Did you know that if you break a cocoon open for a butterfly to help it, it will die? The butterfly has to go through the 'struggle' to become strong enough to break the cocoon open and then be able to fly out as a beautiful New Creation.

It's like when we go through God's Holy Fire to be purified. No one can do it for you. You have to just go through it and let Him purify you, so that you can come out the other side as pure gold, ready to be used as the Lord's vessel to bring Him glory and bring His Kingdom in.

At that moment of my life, I was literally just taking it one day at a time, knowing and trusting that God would get me through every single day by His grace. Trusting the Lord took on a whole new meaning for me when it was the only option I had.

One of the things that helped me a lot through this season was to worship the Lord as much as I could every day. We don't always realise what a powerful weapon worship is in the Spirit realm but things really shift in the atmosphere when you start worshipping the Lord aloud, specifically when you are going through a storm. The enemy surely doesn't like hanging around when you worship.

When your focus is on worshipping God, you can't focus on your feelings and emotions that are usually very up and down when you go through an emotional challenging time. The Holy Spirit led me to a specific worship song, called *It is well with my soul*. I worshipped the Lord with that song over and over daily and I don't believe there's any coincidence that He wanted me to sing those words out into the atmosphere daily. My soul was wounded and I needed to speak and sing God's word over it.

*The Lord is close to the broken-hearted and saves those who are crushed in spirit.*

Psalms 34:18 TPT

# Chapter 2

# Grace

*The Lord answered me, 'My grace is always more than enough for you, and My power finds its full expression through your weakness.' So I will celebrate my weaknesses, for when I'm weak I sense more deeply the mighty power of Christ living in me.*

2 Corinthians 12:9 TPT

At the beginning of 2017 I had booked a holiday for my husband and I to go to my favourite Greek island, Skiathos, for a week. I guess it was the last glimmer of hope I clung onto that, maybe just maybe, we would get through the storm in our marriage.

Skiathos is a place I'd been going to for over 10 years and it's always been very close to my heart. It's a place where I always experience God's presence in a very special deep way and He always speaks to me when I'm out there. It's also very close to Thessaloniki, where there's a lot of Biblical history.

I'd already paid for the holiday in January and because I couldn't get a refund, I decided to still go by myself as

I really needed a holiday away after everything that had been going on.

At the time I booked the holiday, I got a special discounted rate for a room at a hotel right on the beach. I had seen this hotel when I was on holiday before and dreamt of staying there one day but knew it was very expensive. I'd assumed because of the low rate I paid for the room that it would probably be a very small room and probably right at the back of the hotel with no view at all. But at least I'd finally be staying at my dream hotel in Skiathos after all these years, even if it wasn't a nice room…

As the plane landed at Skiathos airport, I felt a big sense of relief. A sense of finally 'being home' in my 'safe happy place' far away from London and all the pain and disappointment of the last 4 years. I got on the usual transfer bus at the airport and within 10 minutes we'd arrived at the hotel. Reception quickly helped me and I was led to my room by a staff member. I was so excited. Finally, I was staying at my dream hotel in Skiathos. As he unlocked the room, I was ready for 'what I'd prepared myself for', but as I walked into my room, I simply didn't have any words – my mouth was literally hanging open….

There in front of me was the complete opposite of what I was expecting. An executive suite with a balcony and as I walked outside, I saw the most beautiful sea view I could have ever wished for. As I was standing there in awe, the tears just welled up in my eyes and started rolling down my cheeks….

I was completely humbled and overwhelmed by God's immense love for me. His love just poured and poured deep into my heart as I was standing on that balcony. As I stood there it felt like the Lord was holding me very tightly in His arms saying 'I love you more than you know my precious daughter. You are mine. You are not alone. I'm with you right by your side.' And the Holy tears just streamed and streamed over my cheeks as He kissed me with His tremendous love.

When His love cascades over you, it brings you into a much deeper intimacy with Him on new levels that you didn't even know existed.

> *Then you will be empowered to discover what every Holy one experiences – the great magnitude of the astonishing love of Christ in all its dimensions. How deeply intimate and far-reaching is His love! How enduring and inclusive it is! Endless love beyond measurement that transcends our understanding – this extravagant love pours into you until you are filled to overflowing with the fullness of God!*

Ephesians 3:18–19 TPT

The Lord's favour was on that holiday from beginning to end. I had time to rest, eat wonderful Greek food and enjoy the sunshine. It felt like every breath I took I was breathing in more healing and restoration into my soul. I was surrounded by His peace and love everywhere.

To make it even better, a good friend ended up joining me for two days right at the end of my holiday, so I was able to show her the island and why I loved it so much.

I also had time to visit the Skiathos cat welfare association to find out more about volunteering later on in the year with this charity that does such amazing work on the island looking after all the stray cats – neutering and rehoming them. The charity requires a lot of work and they always need volunteers to help out with the cats. The management of the stray cats has always been a big challenge on the Greek islands and it really warmed my heart to see such kind-hearted people really caring and making a true difference for the cats in Skiathos.

As my holiday drew to an end, I got on the plane to fly back to the UK and my heart was overflowing with gratitude. I felt a bit more 'ready' to face 'life back in the UK' again. Little did I know what surprise gift the Lord had in store for me when I returned home.

# Chapter 3

# An unexpected gift

*Every gift God freely gives us is good and perfect,*
*streaming down from the Father of Lights, who*
*shines from the heavens with no hidden shadow*
*or darkness and is never subject to change.*

James 1:17 TPT

*If you, imperfect as you are, know how to lovingly*
*take care of your children and give them what's best,*
*how much more ready is your Heavenly Father to*
*give wonderful gifts to those who ask Him?*

Matthew 7:11 TPT

I'll quickly take you back to my childhood years. I was born with a great passion and love for animals that the Lord Himself placed in my heart. For as long as I can remember I've always tried to help animals or save them. The whole Basson family have big hearts for animals and I grew up going on family holidays to the Kruger National Park every June school holiday. Apparently my first trip there happened even before I was a year old.

It was the highlight of the year for our family and the excitement and joy we all experienced from those wonderful times in nature, surrounded by God's beautiful creation were always treasured in our hearts. Our days were filled with early morning game drives, afternoon game drives and barbecues every night. My brother printed lists out for all of us to fill in exactly how many animals we saw on each drive. We would then compare our lists with my aunt and uncle in the evening around the campfire to see who had the 'best/most successful' day on the road spotting animals.

My mum can tell you stories of all the mice I tried to save after rescuing them from my cat when I was little. The next morning my mum would find the mouse (unfortunately dead) lying in a bed of leaves by the front door, with a piece of cheese and a toothpaste lid filled with water next to it – I was always determined that I would save it from dying and that it would still be alive the next morning.

Over the years I've gathered quite a few animal rescue stories, some of them quite comical. I'm the one that would always stop in the middle of traffic and run to help an animal or bird in distress. Those of you that have the same passion will know it's not really something you can control – if you can help an animal you would, no matter what. That's what your heart tells you to do.

I'll share two of my rescue stories. It was a dark, rainy Friday night during winter in Wimbledon, London. I was standing at the bus stop by Wimbledon High Street, when I noticed a pigeon in the road that kept moving very close to the cars and almost getting hit a couple of times. It wasn't long until I realised, I'd have to step in and help. There I was on my way to meet a friend for dinner in Putney, dressed in boots with heels dodging between the traffic trying to catch the pigeon, who seemed to be very confused. Catching a pigeon in the rain with traffic moving on both sides was not the easiest of things to do but, by the grace of God, I managed to catch it. As soon as I did, I looked up and to my surprise all the people at the bus stop started cheering and clapping their hands – this was quite unexpected and funny at the same time.

I jumped into the first black cab I could get with the pigeon inside my jacket. Having a ride in a black cab was probably a first for this London pigeon. I went back home, put the pigeon in my spare room and jumped straight back in another black cab to go meet my friend for dinner. To this day she still brings that story up and still thinks it very funny. The next morning, I took the pigeon to the vets who managed to look after him and help him with the right medication.

Then there was the time when I was at work, looking out of my surgery window inbetween patients, seeing a cat running across one of the countryside roads with something in its mouth. He dropped it and kept moving. Shortly after I saw a magpie coming to sit down next to 'what had dropped out of the cat's mouth'. I couldn't see what it was but decided to quickly run out to have a look. (This was a new job that I only started a couple of weeks before.)

As I moved closer, I saw a tiny baby squirrel on the road. He was moving but couldn't get up and seemed to be injured. I had nothing with me to pick the baby squirrel up with, so I had to pick it up with my bare hands. At that moment, the receptionist turned into the road to park her car. I stopped her and showed her the baby squirrel. I asked if there was maybe vets close by and to my surprise she said 'just around the corner'. I asked her to please take me. I got into the car with the baby squirrel on my lap. What happened next was the last thing I was expecting.

As I was busy admiring this sweet, adorable baby squirrel, it sat up and bit straight into my finger. I gave a loud scream which was followed by a very loud scream by the receptionist. It was extremely painful and the squirrel didn't let go – he latched on and I could actually hear his tooth on the bone of my finger. At that moment I knew I had to pull his little head off my finger, which is what I did and thankfully he did let go. Blood was pouring out of my finger and the pain was quite intense. Luckily, we got to the vets quickly and one of the nurses came to collect the squirrel from me as I was too scared to pick it up encase it bit me again.

I didn't know at the time that baby squirrels have got one big fat tooth and when they bite, they don't let go very easily. We got back to the practice and I had to quickly rush to A&E to get the wound (that was pouring with blood), looked at.

It was a first for the receptionist to have to explain to my dental hygiene patients that I wouldn't be in for the rest of the afternoon due to being bitten by a baby squirrel.

The receptionist at A&E found my story very funny and the doctor actually told me how she also got bitten in her shoulder trying to keep a squirrel away from her dog.

If you would ask me whether I would help that little baby squirrel again if I was in the same situation, I absolutely would, but I would definitely first get some clothing or a towel to wrap it in, so it couldn't bite me.

After returning home from Skiathos, I invited some old friends to come for a barbecue and stay the night. They lived quite far away from me, a good two-hour drive, and I was quite excited to spend some time with dear friends, seeing that I didn't have any friends in the area I lived in.

On the day, I had everything ready waiting for them to arrive when their plans suddenly changed very unexpectedly and they had to make a U-turn and go back home due to a family member's flight being cancelled. I remember feeling quite disappointed thinking *it's going to be another quiet weekend. Just myself and my dear Simba, (my rescue cat).*

I adopted Simba from Battersea dog and cat shelter in London on my birthday in 2013. It was exactly 6 months after I lost my dear Toffee, who was also a rescue ginger cat from Battersea. I was so heartbroken after Toffee suddenly died of kidney failure after being with me for 5 years. I didn't think I would get another cat after losing Toffee but somehow I found myself at Battersea a day before my birthday just to have a 'look' to see whether there might be a cat that chose me.

I remember it was the very last glass compartment that I walked to and to my disappointment there was no cat inside. The lady showing me, said Simba was very traumatised and scared of people due to the way he was treated before. He was only 1 year old and he wouldn't come out of his carry cage. I decided to go inside and see if he would come closer. Just thinking of the first time I looked into his eyes, makes my eyes fill up with tears. I could see so much pain and emptiness in those eyes. He had no confidence and I couldn't help but wonder what on earth his previous owners had done to him that after only 1 year, he looked like this.

I started stroking him and talking to him. After a good while I could sense that he felt safe with me. He walked out of his cage for me to stroke him and quickly walked back in again. And just there and then I knew 'Simba, my beautiful boy, today you have found your mum'.

And what a privilege it's been to have seen the enormous transformation in my Simba's life just from giving him a safe loving home. He's so beautiful – ginger and white with long hair. He makes me laugh all the time as he's so funny, playful and full of personality. I couldn't imagine life without him.

So, as I was feeling a bit low after hearing my friends couldn't visit anymore, I decided to go for a long run. Little did I know what would happen when I got home...

As I walked over to the kitchen and looked out to my back garden, I suddenly saw two little eyes looking straight at me from between my flowerpots. At first, I wasn't sure what it was, maybe a small squirrel? As I walked outside, to my surprise I saw it was a very tiny baby wild rabbit. I'd never seen such a small rabbit before and quickly went inside to find a container to put her in so I could help her. As I gently put her inside the container, she just fell over. At that very moment, the Holy Spirit told me to pick her up and put her inside my top so that she could hear my heartbeat and stay warm. I picked her up and put this tiny adorable little rabbit inside my top and she immediately fell fast asleep.

As I was standing there in absolute awe of what had just happened the Lord said to me 'Her name is Gracy'. In that moment, as I looked at her and my heart completely melted, I knew this was way more than just a baby rabbit... This was a gift. It was a complete mystery as to how she got there on her own away from her mum, between my flowerpots. The garden was completely blocked off and there was just no way for her to end up there. To this day I believe it was an angel that brought her and placed her there.

As I was standing there admiring this precious baby rabbit sleeping in my top, I knew that although she would not have made it through another day on her own without food, water or protection, I needed her way more than she needed me...

That was the day I became Gracy's mum.

And all of a sudden my heart was flooded with so much love towards this adorable little baby rabbit, Gracy. It felt like my heart wanted to burst with love for her.

I quickly got a box and made her a soft cosy bed. That afternoon I rushed to the shop to get some pellets and hay for her. By the evening I realised she couldn't actually eat or drink on her own, as she was way too small and needed to be fed with a syringe.

The Holy Spirit reminded me of an old South African friend that's a vet in the UK, so I quickly contacted her and she told me to get full cream goats milk and feed Gracy three to four times a day with a small syringe but to do it very slowly so that she wouldn't get aspiration pneumonia. I had no idea that a lot of baby wild rabbits don't always make it when being hand raised due to stress, not being fed the right milk and not being fed slowly.

I was determined to help her as best I could. I knew that God's grace would help me through it and the Holy Spirit would guide me with wisdom on what to do.

All of a sudden, my husband and all the negative memories were far from my mind and my focus was on one thing and one thing alone and that was helping Baby Gracy to eat and become strong and healthy. My heart was full of love for this little vulnerable baby rabbit and nothing was going to stop me from helping her.

Inside I was bursting with excitement. My heart felt like it was beating again. It was wonderful to feel so much love after love not being present for such a long time.

All of a sudden, I felt a sense of purpose again.

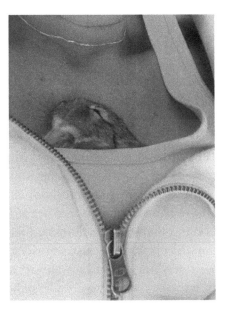

# Chapter 4

# Gracy's first month

I can still remember the excitement and nervousness I felt the first time I fed Gracy with the goats milk using a small syringe. I knew I had to take my time and only give her very small amounts at a time so that it didn't get into her lungs. Many baby rabbits die when being hand raised as a result of aspiration pneumonia caused when they are being fed too quickly and milk ends up in their lungs. The sense of relief after giving her that first syringe of milk successfully was just wonderful.

And how she loved her goats milk. It was so wonderful to watch this adorable little baby rabbit drinking her milk and being so at peace in my hand. A little bundle of sweetness and love that stole her mum's heart. I felt like my heart was smiling every time I looked at her.

It was 4 weeks in total of feeding Gracy three to four times a day until she started drinking and eating on her own. I used to set my alarm an hour earlier in the mornings to have enough time to feed her at 5:00 before going to work and then rush back in my lunch break to feed her again. Sleep was the last priority during that first month of feeding her. Everyone at work knew about Gracy and they were very understanding about

me having to rush out before lunch to make it back in time for work after feeding her. Every day that went by she became stronger and grew cuter and cuter. Each day felt like a victory and I fell more in love with her every day. I couldn't wait to get home and check on her to see her adorable little face.

All of a sudden feeding times became my favourite time of the day. She would make the cutest little noises when drinking and have a little 'goats milk moustache' afterwards.

One month later I started putting some pellets in a little bowl and some goats milk next to it in another bowl. What a great moment it was when she started eating and drinking on her own – I felt like a proud mum whose baby had just started crawling. I started to introduce water with a bit of goats milk in a separate bowl next to it, before slowly weaning her off the goats milk entirely and onto pellets, water and hay.

It was summer in the UK with nice long days. For me it was very important to take Gracy out daily for at least 2–3 hours. Simba always came to join us outside. He was actually unaware of Gracy for the first couple of weeks while I was carrying her around with me. It was quite funny when I introduced Simba for the first time to her. Gracy was full of energy hopping around in the house and when Simba saw her, he got quite a fright. He had never seen anything like it before and I guess he didn't know what to make of her. She on the other hand, had no fear of anything whatsoever, so she just ran straight up to him and looked him in the eyes. Simba felt very uncomfortable and immediately jumped away.

For me it was always very adorable that from the start, Gracy used to always get a little bit jealous (in a very sweet way) if Simba would get near me and she would look directly at me as if to say 'You're MY mom. I'm not sure what he's doing here'.

From the start I never left the two of them alone, because I couldn't risk Simba maybe wanting to play with her and hurting or scratching her through playing with her. I also knew in my heart, because Gracy was so special and a wild rabbit, I would never want to expose her unnecessarily to vets, operations or sedations. The stress alone of a situation like that would do more harm than good.

I waited until she was a couple of months old and registered her at my local vet. I made sure it was the very last appointment of the day and stayed in the car until they called me, to not let Gracy get stressed unnecessary. It was so wonderful to see their reaction. They all said how beautiful she was. They were amazed and said they don't often see a wild rabbit surviving being hand raised. Even just the stress alone can kill them. I told them I got a lot of God's grace to raise her. My house was also very quiet and peaceful, so it was ideally a stress-free environment for her.

The amazing thing was that I didn't know whether Gracy was male or female when I got her, but the Lord told me her name is Gracy and I knew she was a girl. At the vets I asked them to please check for me what her gender was and they confirmed 'it's a girl'.

When I asked them how long a wild rabbit's lifespan was, they said in the wild usually not more than a year, due to all the predators such as eagles and foxes. But if she's in a safe secure environment, she could live up to five or six years. For me, every day with her, was a gift. I knew God had a reason for bringing her into my life and He would take her back home to Him when her season with me was over.

Once a year the vets would contact me to remind me about Gracy's yearly vaccination. We were usually in and out of there in 10 minutes. I would take the last appointment of the day and wait in the car with her till they were ready. We kept it as stress free as possible but to be honest it was more stressful for me because I didn't want her to feel scared at all. She was always super happy when we got home where she felt safe.

The vet mentioned to me during her first appointment that I should think about sterilising Gracy, because sometimes female rabbits could develop cancer in the womb if not sterilised. For me it was not an option to put her through that as a wild rabbit. I chose to ask God to protect her and keep her healthy for as long as it was His will. Every morning when I got up, I covered myself, Gracy, Simba and my family with the Blood of Jesus and believed we were all protected.

*And now we are brothers and sisters in God's family because of the blood of Jesus, and He welcomes us to come into the most holy Sanctuary in the heavenly realm-boldly and without hesitation.*

Hebrews 10:19

*Just as the mountains surround Jerusalem, so the Lord's wraparound presence surrounds his people, protecting them now and forever.*

Psalm 125:2 TPT

# Chapter 5

# New doors opening

We had a great summer that year. Life seemed wonderfully simple and peaceful after the 'storm' I'd been through in my marriage.

I never expected a baby wild rabbit to have so much personality. Gracy brought joy and love to me every single day. There was not one day where she didn't make me smile or laugh aloud. Alongside her incredible cuteness, she was incredibly smart and funny and we grew closer every single day. Being her mum, was an absolute joy and I showered her with love every day.

Simba and I would sit daily outside with Gracy for at least 3–4 hours while she was in her playpen and evenings were spent inside.

All the hurt and disappointment of my marriage was very far removed from me as my whole focus was now on being the best mum I could possibly be for my little angel Gracy.

The Lord used her like a 'healing balm' for my heart, and slowly but surely my heart started recovering day by day through His love and grace.

*He heals the wounds of every shattered heart. He sets his stars in place, calling them all by their names. How great is our God! There's absolutely nothing His power cannot accomplish, and He has infinite understanding of everything.*

Psalm 147:3–5 TPT

As the months went by, the cost of the house that I was in became too high for me to cover on my own and around the same time I lost two of the days that I had been working at the dental practice as they didn't have enough patients to keep me busy.

I prayed and asked the Lord to firstly make a way for me, Gracy and Simba to find a new home that would cost less, have a bigger garden for Gracy's playpen and also a spare room for Gracy's cage and secondly to give me a new job that would be closer to home and that would pay me better than the job I had before.

All of a sudden uncertainty was staring me in the face again but I knew I had only one option and that was to keep my eyes on Jesus, who is faithful and who I trust with all my heart to provide and make a way for me when nobody else can.

So, as I was driving home one day, I passed a dental practice in a small little town close to where I live and decided to stop, go inside and leave my details in case they might be looking for a dental hygienist. As I walked in and started talking to the receptionist, I got a good first impression of the practice. She said she will pass my details on to the owner as their current hygienist was leaving soon and they would be looking for a replacement. As I drove away with a smile on my face, I just knew 'Jesus got this'. I didn't need to worry at all.

*Pour out all your worries and stress upon him and leave them there, for he always tenderly cares for you.*

1 Peter 5:7 TPT

And it wasn't long after that that I got the phone call asking me to come in for an interview for the new job. I went for the interview feeling at peace and as soon as I had left I was pretty certain I got the job. Later that afternoon I got the phone call to confirm that I had indeed got the job. Not only was this job much closer to where I lived but they had also offered me a better salary. My heart was overflowing with joy and gratitude towards the Lord. He did it. He answered my prayers. All glory to Him. Grace and favour from my faithful Lord Jesus.

Soon after that I started looking online for available properties to rent in my area. I saw a house that the Holy Spirit highlighted to me and I was immediately drawn to it. I got in my car and drove to the street to have a look at the house from the outside. I had a peace in my heart about the location and called immediately to arrange a viewing. The viewing was booked in a couple of days and I was super excited. I couldn't afford a deposit for renting a new house and this house had a 'no deposit scheme' which meant no upfront deposit was needed. I didn't even know that you could get an option like that at the time, but again the Lord made a way and showed me I didn't have to worry about the deposit.

*Refuse to worry about tomorrow but deal with each challenge that comes your way, one day at a time. Tomorrow will take care of itself.*

Matthew 6:34 TPT

On the day of the viewing, I got to the house to find a couple waiting outside. I had been expecting to view the house on my own but they were also booked in to view the house at the same time as me. Immediately I felt intimidated as they had two salaries coming in and I only had one. I kept praying asking the Lord, 'please let me get this house Lord'.

We waited for what seemed like an hour before the estate agent came to open the house to show us. As the couple walked in they were blown away from the start, saying 'Oh this is amazing. It's just perfect for us.' I knew in my heart, that it would take a miracle from God for me to get the house as otherwise it just seemed completely impossible. I walked through the house thinking to myself, 'this is even better than what I saw on the photos' but the best part was when the estate agent opened the back door to take us to the back garden. There had been no photos of the back garden at all in the advertisement that I had seen online, so what I saw next was just beyond anything I was expecting. As I walked out behind the couple, I saw one enormous, beautiful garden, divided into a big patio area and an even bigger grass section with lots of big trees. The Lord knows how much I love nature and big trees. And not only that, but the garden was also south-facing, which meant it got a lot of sun.

As the couple walked further down the garden in absolute awe, I said to the estate agent 'What now? They clearly want the house and I also want it. What do I do?' She told me to call the estate agent's office as soon as I left the house and tell them that I wanted it. She couldn't guarantee me that I would get it as it would be up to the landlord to decide.

I left the house, got into my car and said, 'Lord I love this house, I really want it. Please help me to get it. Only you can make this happen.'

I phoned the estate agent office and told them that I had viewed the house and I wanted it. They said they would speak to the landlord and would let me know what he said. I drove away saying, 'Lord this is all in your hands. All I can do now, is trust that you will make a way'.

I drove to the big supermarket a couple of blocks away and decided to do my food shopping. No more than

15 minutes after I left the house my phone rang. It was the estate agent. She said 'It's yours. The landlord said you can have the house.'

Have you ever had one of those 'jaw-dropping moments'? This was one of them for me. All I could get out of my mouth was 'Wow, Lord, Wow. Thank you, thank you, thank you...' I knew that it was God, and only God, who made this possible and I was in absolute awe. It was His Favour, and His Favour alone, that made a way for me.

> *Lord, how wonderfully you bless the righteous. Your favour wraps around each one and covers them under your canopy of kindness and joy.*

> Psalms 5:12 TPT

I was immediately filled with so much excitement. A new start in a new home. The other house had lots of bad memories from when my husband was there and this new house would mean a new start and new happy memories in a new season of my life. Finally, there would be nothing to remind me of the past.

The house was available to move into from the end of September. I contacted the estate agents in charge of my current house and they told me that I would still need to pay an extra month's rent after I'd moved out unless I could find tenants to move in when I moved out.

So, yet another obstacle suddenly in the way… There was no way I could afford to pay rent at the new house as well as pay for the house I was moving out of. I needed another miracle and went straight to God. 'Lord, I believe this is the house you have for me. You have made a way that I could get it. Please send me tenants that can move into my current house end of September when I'm moving out.'

This seemed like a complete impossibility but I decided to trust God. He made a way before, so He would do it again. And slowly God started to pull me closer and deeper into trusting Him, when trusting Him was the only option I had.

And as I got to know Him as faithful and good, His faithfulness came through once again making a way where there was no way. A couple of people came to have a look at the house but then I got the call from a lady who was really desperate. Their house had flooded about 3 weeks ago and they were stuck in a hotel until their house got fixed. They were desperate to get out and as the insurance were going to cover their costs, they were looking for somewhere to rent for 6 months while the repairs on their house were completed.

I could not have asked for more. Again, I was just blown away and in awe of God 'making a way for me'.

*…And now we have run into His heart to hide ourselves in His faithfulness. This is where we find His strength and comfort, for He empowers*

*us to seize what has already been established ahead of time – an unshakeable hope!*

Hebrews 6:18 TPT

The big packing and clearing session started. I had a house full of furniture that belonged to my husband and as he wasn't interested in collecting it, I had to somehow get rid of it all as I was moving into a furnished house. Again though, as big as the task looked in the natural to do on my own, I wasn't on my own and the Lord helped me all the way to get it all done, one step at a time. As I was packing the last of my stuff, I looked up at the chandelier... and I was taken back to the day my husband and I went to look for the right one. I was so excited to get a chandelier and took my time to choose the best one that would just look so beautiful and make a real difference to the whole room. I remember my husband installing it and me being so happy and excited to switch it on for the first time. Yet here I was looking at the same chandelier, knowing that I had no idea how to dismantle it and had no choice but to leave it behind...

There's a reason I'm telling you about this chandelier and that's to show you how Jesus sees and knows everything about us. He is interested in the finest details of our lives, even if it's something as insignificant and as simple as a chandelier.

And finally the day arrived for me, Simba and Gracy to start a new life in our new house. I remember that first day in my new home, the home that the Lord chose for me. I felt so loved and in awe of my Lord, my Way maker Jesus.

I started seeing all the finer details that I hadn't seen before when I came to quickly view the house. As I noticed all these finer details and realised it's all the little things that I really liked, I realised more and more that this wasn't just another house but this was a house that Jesus had handpicked for me for this season of my life.

As well as the beautiful big garden, there was so much more to this house. The Lord alone knew how much I loved a fireplace and I had never had one in any of the homes I lived in for 20 years. This house had not one but two beautiful fireplaces; one in the living room and one in the dining room. The cushions on the chairs had wild rabbits on them. There was a big glass door where I could see the beautiful back garden from my living room. The bedrooms had big windows (I love big windows and lots of natural light). There was a beautiful chandelier in the living room and when I looked up at the second chandelier in the dining room, I paused for a moment... All of a sudden my eyes filled up with tears as I stood there looking at the exact same chandelier that I had to leave behind in the previous house... and in that moment I knew how much My Father loved me and how the finer details in our lives really matter to Him...

*I love each of you with the same love that the Father loves me. You must continually let my love nourish your hearts.*

John 15:9 TPT

35

And so I felt Jesus's love for me coming from all directions through Simba, Gracy and my beautiful new home. I felt content, at peace and loved as His love nourished my heart.

Gracy was now about 5 months old and full of energy and personality. I couldn't wait to build her new playpen outside in my big new garden. I ended up buying three playpens that I combined into one big playpen. The Holy Spirit gave me wisdom to put a big net over the top, so that if she did jump, she wouldn't get hurt.

And how she loved spending time outside daily in her playpen. Simba loved his new garden too and although I kept him inside the house for the first month, he enjoyed every moment exploring his new surroundings.

I soon realised that Gracy loved the grass being a bit longer in her playpen so that she could play around

and hide in it. So I made sure I didn't cut the grass too often.

Initially it was quite a challenge to catch her but through the Lord's grace I developed the skill needed to be able to catch her every time it was time to take her back inside. She was so clever and knew as soon as I got into the playpen, it was time to go inside. It was almost like a little game to her and I'm sure it was a bit funny for her to watch her mum trying to catch her. But as soon as we were inside, she would be so happy and would sit washing herself from head to toe. I loved watching her when she did that. My favourite bit was when she washed her little face with her little white fluffy paws and then started cleaning behind those cute little ears. I never knew that rabbits actually clean themselves just like cats do.

Everyone in my life knew about Gracy and they always wanted to know how she was doing. I was very protective over her and it was very important to me that she always felt loved and safe. People didn't always understand that she was very different from a normal rabbit. That she would always be a wild rabbit even though I hand raised her. They wanted to see her and pick her up or stroke her but that was simply not possible.

The daughter of a good friend of mine came over one day and of course she wanted to see and stroke Gracy. That was the day I realised that it would be the very last time I would allow anyone except myself or a vet near her.

I kept Gracy in her cage and stroked her first and closed her eyes so she didn't get a fright when she saw the girl. The girl softly started to stroke her, but immediately Gracy picked up it was a different scent that wasn't mine and she got scared. I asked the girl to please leave the room immediately and I calmed Gracy down. I felt so much guilt for making her feel unsafe in her own home. She got lots of love and cuddles from her mum afterwards and, after apologising to her, I promised her that I would never let anyone except her vet close to touch her again.

My beautiful darling angel Gracy.

# Chapter 6

# Holy Spirit encounters

It was our first winter in our new home. When I wasn't at work, Simba and I were either outside with Gracy by her playpen or the three of us would be inside downstairs where Gracy could run around, Simba would be sleeping and I would be listening to worship music, worship or online faith teachings.

I couldn't get enough of growing and learning more about God. The Lord started to stir up a great passion and a fire in my heart to pursue Him and all that He had for me that was at a much greater level than before.

At that stage I'd been what you would call a 'Christian' my whole life. I grew up in a Christian home with my dad being the Minister of a Dutch Reformed Church in South Africa. I went to church twice on a Sunday with my mum and brother while my dad would preach. It was only much later on in life, at the age of 30, that I went to a Spirit-filled church in London and felt the presence of The Holy Spirit for the very first time.

It was such a tangible presence that I couldn't wait to go again the following Sunday. It was all new to me and for 2 years I sat on my own on the balcony of Holy Trinity

Brompton in Knightsbridge every Sunday, experiencing the presence of the Lord and watching His Holy Spirit move in the service. I was fascinated. How could it be that this was completely missing from what I thought church was supposed to be like, growing up as a Minister's child...?

*Beloved ones, God has called us to live a life of freedom in the Holy Spirit.*

Gal 5:13 TPT

I am blessed with a wonderful mum and dad whom I dearly love with all my heart. They have always supported and loved me no matter what.

I can remember how at times while I was growing up my parents would have conversations with each other regarding people being baptised at a later stage in life (what we call being baptised by the Holy Spirit) and speaking in tongues. This was always discussed in a negative tone and it was very clear to me from a young age that my parents didn't approve of it and thought it would be wrong to be baptised by the Holy Spirit or speak in tongues. The Dutch Reformed Church didn't approve of the Baptism of the Holy Spirit.

It's now that I can reflect back and see that I grew up in a very 'religious church environment' and that the baptism of the Holy Spirit was not part of this environment. Miracles and the Power of the Holy Spirit were something I had never seen or experienced in church until I moved to the UK in 2000 and I started to experience the Holy Spirit for the first time at Holy Trinity Brompton. The Lord started to slowly but surely draw me closer and closer to him, wanting more.

So although I grew up in an 'Christian environment', I wasn't walking in the 'fullness' of what the Lord had planned for me and I started realising that there was more. That Jesus still performs miracles, heals and delivers today, just like He did in the Bible.

*Jesus, the Anointed One, is always the same – yesterday, and today, and forever.*

Hebrews 13:8 TPT

It was about 2 years after I started going to Holy Trinity Brompton, when I was driving home from work one day that I had a life changing encounter with the Holy Spirit, that changed and 'marked' me forever.

I was listening to my worship CD as I was driving home after work and I was singing *From the inside out* by Hillsong with a passion that came straight from my heart. As I sang the line *Holy Spirit consume me from the inside out'* while driving through Richmond Park, all of a sudden the Holy Spirit responded in power by touching me and consuming me right there in my car. It was so unexpected and powerful. It was like He baptised me in His fire and love all at once. As it happened, I immediately burst into tears and started crying uncontrollably while driving all the way home. Even when I arrived home, I sat in my car and couldn't stop crying for about 20 minutes. The Lord kept pouring and pouring into me. I knew the Lord was busy doing a great work in me, healing my heart by His power and this was a supernatural act by His Spirit.

This was the very first time I ever had such a powerful encounter with the Holy Spirit. I was in awe.

*Not by Might, not by power but by My Spirit, says the Lord Almighty.*

Zachariah 4:1

From that day on things started to change in my life and the Lord started to steer me in the right direction. Slowly He started removing the 'weeds' in my life, one by one and very gently.

I remember how He started to speak to me in my dreams. I specifically remember the night I asked Him for the very first time to speak to me through a dream.

At that point I'd been in a relationship with a guy for many years that wasn't good for me. The enemy worked hard to try and keep me in that relationship through manipulation and control but that night as I asked the Lord to please show me what to do, He spoke to me. I had not been expecting Him to answer my prayer

42

immediately. I thought He might speak to me through a dream maybe in a couple of weeks, maybe in a month but no that night He answered me. And His message was as clear as daylight to me.

I dreamt I was walking on a beach. It was a beautiful day and I saw a beautiful house build on the sand very close to the water. It looked like the perfect house and I could see inside it, the happy married couple and their dog, a Golden Retriever. It all looked so perfect... but then all of a sudden, the water started to rise and the waves started to come in. The rain and the wind came and the waves got bigger and bigger. I watched how this house was being washed away bit by bit as the waves crashed against it and the sand started giving way under it, it was all destroyed right in front of me. It was so clear; I remember it like it was yesterday. And the Lord said to me, 'My daughter, build your life on Me as the foundation and your future will be secure'.

*Everyone then who hears these words of mine and does them will be like a wise man who built his house on a rock. And the rain fell and the floods came, and the winds blew and beat on that house but it did not fall, because it had been founded in a rock. And everyone who hears these words and does not do them, will be like a foolish man who built his house in the sand. And the rain came, and the winds blew and beat against the house, and it fell, and great was the fall of it.*

Matthew 7:24–26 ESV

This dream spoke straight into my heart and the Lord in His mercy gave me another dream that same night to address the relationship I was in. In this dream He referred to this boyfriend of mine as a big black snake that I was carrying around with me in a box. It was dark, at night and I was very scared of the snake. I threw the box down to walk away from it but then I felt sorry for the snake and walked back to pick the box up again, although I was still scared of it.

The Lord could not have spoken more clearly to me. I was in a dark relationship where I tried several times to break up with this person but the enemy kept manipulating me to feel sorry for him and take him back.

After that dream I knew exactly what to do and ended the relationship without hesitating.

And so my journey of walking with the Lord in a much closer, deeper relationship began. And since that moment I had a hunger to see His miracles happen. And I started seeing them...

So back to Gracy's first winter in our new home. One evening I witnessed firsthand how the Lord performed a miracle right in front of my eyes. It was cold and I was woken from a deep sleep in the middle of the night. I heard the Holy Spirit telling me to go to Gracy in her room immediately. I felt quite uneasy but got up and went straight there.

When I got to her cage, I took her out and could immediately see something was terribly wrong. My heart literally felt as if it tightened when I saw her. To this day I'm not sure what was happening at that moment but from what I could see, she looked like she was dying. She was very cold and didn't respond. Absolute panic kicked in and I started calling out to God while the tears started streaming down my face. I held her in my hands and kept pleading 'God please save her. Please save her Jesus. Help her, help her Jesus'.

I kept saying it over and over again and could not stop crying. I couldn't tell for how long I stood there sobbing in between pleading with the Lord to save Gracy, but it felt like at least 40 min of crying, praying and pleading with the Lord to help and intervene. Then, all of a sudden... The only way I can describe it is that it was like some sort of an electric shock hit her and she jumped straight up and was 100% normal...

I wish I could've seen my face at that moment, my mouth must've been literally hanging open. There, in front of my eyes, I saw how the Lord intervened with his Holy Spirit power to save Gracy. I held her and stroked her and she looked at me as if to say 'Mum, why have you been crying? What's wrong?'

It took me quite a while to fall back to sleep that night as I was trying to get my head around what just happened. I saw a true miracle. My Faithful Jesus had heard my prayers and He intervened and saved her. I was in awe...

*I promise you, if you have faith inside of you no bigger than the size of a small mustard seed, you can say to this mountain, 'Move away from here and go over there' and you will see it move!*

Matthew 17:20 TPT

From that day on, after experiencing what the Holy Spirit did right in front of my eyes, my faith moved to a complete new level and I knew in my heart that with God absolutely nothing was impossible.

I wanted to taste and experience everything that was on the Lord's table for me, not just one thing but everything – all the signs, wonders and miracles. I wanted to walk in the fullness of what it meant to be His daughter. And deep in my heart the desire for the gift of healing started to grow slowly but surely stronger and stronger.

*A Spiritual gift is given to each of us as a means of helping the entire church.*

1 Corinthians 12:7 TPT

*He knows we are His since He has also stamped His seal of love over our hearts and has given us the Holy Spirit like an engagement ring is given to a bride – a down payment of the blessings to come.*

2 Corinthians 1:22 TPT

It was probably about a month later. Life was wonderful and I kept growing in my relationship with the Lord daily. Then all of a sudden, I got a phone call with news that I was not expecting at all…

From the moment my husband and I separated, I firmly kept believing with my whole heart that somehow the Lord would intervene. That my husband would give his heart to the Lord and that the Lord would bring us back together. I believed this without any doubt in my mind, until I got that phone call…

A good friend of mine was going to see my husband on a weekend away with other friends. I started to get a very uneasy feeling on the Sunday that something wasn't right. I didn't hear back from her, which made me feel even more uneasy, until she phoned me and told me the news…. To this day I'm so grateful that she had the courage to be honest with me and tell me the truth. I remember how in that moment when she told me, my heart broke. He had moved on and was already living with his new girlfriend.

Everything went quiet on the inside of me. It felt like everything came to a standstill… I cried a lot that evening and couldn't even speak to the Lord. I had no words…

It was a couple of days later that I started asking the Lord questions. I knew in that moment the enemy had one big smile on his face. He wanted me to turn from God. He kept whispering in my ear 'How could your God whom you believe in do this to you after you've been believing that He would come through for you…?'

> *Be self-controlled and alert. Your enemy, the devil, prowls around like a roaring lion looking for someone to devour.*

> 1 Peter 5:8 TPT

I thank Jesus for His grace that I very quickly realised I didn't need to have all the answers and I didn't need to understand. All I really needed, was to keep trusting Jesus, knowing deep in my heart He knows everything and He only wants what's best for me and most importantly that He loves me more than I could ever know.

> '*My thoughts about mercy are not like your thoughts, and my ways are different from yours. As high as the heavens are above the earth, so My ways and thoughts are higher than yours.*'

> Isaiah 55:8-9 TPT

That was the day that I stepped into an even deeper level of trust with the Lord, knowing that as long as I'm with Him, He would work everything out in my life. I just needed to trust Him. So I did and His peace and love that surpasses all understanding flooded me.

*For I know the plans I have for you, declares the Lord, plans to prosper you and not to harm you, plans to give you a hope and a future.*

Jeremiah 29:11 TPT

*So we are convinced that every detail of our lives is continually woven together for good, for we are His lovers who have been called to fulfil His designed purpose.*

Romans 8:28 TPT

# Chapter 7

# Abundance

It was June 2018 when I went to South Africa for a short visit for my mum's 70th birthday. It was a wonderful day spent with family and close friends. We all had brunch together at a beautiful venue in Still Bay on the East Coast.

My brother, who's an Internist in Cape Town, also came along with my sister-in-law. My brother has always been gifted in speaking without even preparing. We were about to get in the car to leave for the venue, when he scrambled around to find a piece of paper to quickly write his speech. That's how I know him, so it didn't bother or worry me in the least. And, as usual, he made a beautiful speech in front of everyone honouring my mum on her special birthday.

It's times like that, where it's so important to me to be there to share in the moment and to be making new family memories.

The weekend was over in a flash and the next morning I was off to the beach on the east side for my usual early morning walk that I always treasured in my heart. I've always loved that beach. It's a long white sandy beach and it's on that beach where the Lord often chose to speak to me, when my mind was quiet and when I was at peace and content. But on this specific morning I had no idea what was about to happen and what truth He wanted to reveal to me.

For as long as I can remember I'd walked on that beach hoping to find a whole Pansy shell that's not broken. Since I was a little girl, I'd wanted to find one.

There's something very special about a Pansy shell. It's got a beautiful flower on the front and it's very delicate, but there's so much more to it. It's what the Pansy shell represents that really matters.

The Pansy shell tells the story of the birth of Jesus, the cross and Resurrection.

This little poem describes the meaning of the Pansy shell beautifully.

### The Pansy Shell

There's a lovely little legend
That's always good to tell
Of the birth and death of Jesus
Found in this special shell.

If you look at it quite closely
You'll see that you find here
Four nail holes and a fifth one
Made by the Roman spear.

On one side is the Easter lily
It's centre is the star
That appeared to the waiting shepherds
And led them from afar.

The shape of the poinsettia
Etched on the other side
Reminds us of His birthday,
Our happy Christmas tide.

Now break the centre open
And here you will release
The five white doves awaiting
To speak goodwill and peace

This precious little symbol
God made for you and me
To help us spread His gospel
Through all eternity.

Author unknown

That morning as I started walking on the beach, I thought the same thought I'd thought every time I'd walked there for the last 35 years – 'Would today be the day that I've been waiting for to find my whole Pansy shell?' And as I walked the Holy Spirit whispered gently in my ear 'Ask me for one'.

And immediately I did. I said 'Lord you alone know how special the Pansy shell is to me and for how many years I've been walking on this beach looking for one that's not broken. Please help me find that whole Pansy shell today'.

And I kept walking. As I walked, I saw many broken Pansy shells. At one point I found a fairly big one that had just a single piece missing and I thought to myself *maybe I should just be happy with this* broken one... then the doubt crept in and I thought *it has never happened before, so what difference does it make if I don't find one today? I should just accept what I got although it wasn't what I wanted....*

After walking on the beach for almost an hour and a half, I was getting closer to the point where I had to walk back to my car. I thought *let me just keep looking.*

And then...

There in front of me, as the water pulled back with the tide into the ocean, I saw the face of a Pansy hidden under the sand.

My heart jumped and I kneeled down and scooped the shell up with all the sand covering it. At this point I didn't know if it was a whole Pansy shell, because of all the sand. I was super careful because it was a small Pansy and they break very easily. So I went to the water and gently washed the sand away. And there in front of me in my hand was my very first perfect whole Pansy shell...

I was in absolute awe! Finally, it had happened but more so I knew that this was not a coincidence. There was way more to this... This was God trying to tell me something

53

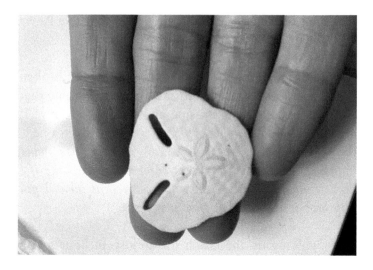

– that if I wanted something all I needed to do was ask Him and have faith that He would give it to me...

> But if you live in life-union with me and if my words live powerfully within you-then you can ask whatever you desire and it will be done. When your lives bear abundant fruit, you will demonstrate that you are my mature disciples who glorify my Father!
>
> John 15:7-8 TPT

> For here is eternal truth: When that time comes you won't need to ask me for anything but instead you will go directly to the Father and ask Him for anything you desire and He will give it to you, because of your relationship with Me.
>
> John 16:23 TPT

Not only was this a perfect whole Pansy shell but it was a very small one, which makes the odds of finding one by the water even smaller. They are so fragile, it's almost impossible for such a small one not to get smashed by the incoming waves and water. The Lord said to me, 'Nothing is impossible for me my daughter.'

So the next morning I went for another walk on that beach. I was still trying to process what had happened the day before and how clearly the Lord spoke to me. I knew that truth needed to take root in my life. As I started walking on the beach and praying, the Lord said to me, 'Ask me again'. I was taken by surprise but immediately asked Him again 'Lord please give me another perfect Pansy shell today'. I could feel the excitement rising up inside of me as I kept walking and praying...

When I was on my way back, I suddenly saw a Pansy shell right in front of me on the sand as the water pulled away. I quickly picked it up and was filled with overflowing excitement. As I stood there looking at it in amazement, the Holy Spirit led me to look to my left and there in front of me was another one! I couldn't believe what was happening. I gently picked it up and saw it was perfect. As I stood up and looked at both Pansy shells, the Lord led me to look a little bit closer to the water. And there in the water in front of me was a third whole Pansy shell!

I wish I could've seen my own face at that moment. There I was, standing with three perfectly whole pansy shells in my hands and as I stared at them, the Holy Spirit said to me 'You ask me for so little, my daughter, but I have abundance for you and I want to give it all to you. I am the Lord of overflow abundance'.

*The enemy comes to steal, kill and destroy but I have come to give you life and give it to you abundantly.*

John 10:10 TPT

It was a life-changing moment for me as the Lord spoke this truth about abundance straight into my heart. It was a truth that I wasn't familiar with. With my upbringing in a Dutch Reformed Church, I somehow believed that prosperity didn't come from God. That, in fact, being very rich and living in overflow abundance was frowned upon by God. Yet here He was speaking to me on a beautiful early morning on the beach in Still Bay, saying the exact opposite. That in fact He IS the God of abundance!

This was a revelation that I knew I had to make a part of myself. I had to renew my mind with it so that the truth could replace the lie that I'd believed for most of my life.

*Every spiritual blessing in the heavenly realm has already been lavished upon us as a love gift from our Heavenly Father, the Father of our Lord Jesus – all because He sees us wrapped into*

*Christ. This is why we celebrate Him with all our hearts.*

Ephesians 1:3 TPT

*Every field is watered with the abundance of rain-showers soaking the earth and softening it clods, causing seeds to sprout throughout the land. You crown the year with its yearly harvest, the fruits of your goodness. Wherever you go the tracks of your chariot wheels drip with oil.*

Psalms 65:10–11 TPT

*Yes God is more than ready to overwhelm you with every form of Grace, so that you will have more than enough of everything – every moment and in every way. He will make you overflow with abundance in every good thing that you do.*

2 Corinthians 9:8 TPT

*The lovers of God who chase after righteousness will find all their dreams come true. An abundant life drenched with favour and a fountain that overflows with satisfaction.*

Proverbs 21:21 TPT

When I got back home I started to look for a Spirit filled church local to where I lived and it quickly became very clear that there wasn't a lot of Spirit filled churches around at all.

I remember the one evening I went to a church in Guildford for the first time. I will never forget that night. I sat in that church and it was so clear that the Holy Spirit wasn't present at all. It was a religious church and the Lord's Spirit was not present...

I kept looking at the clock and considered walking out but waited till the end and left filled with a lot of disappointment. As I was driving home, I said to myself 'I will never in my life waste my time again sitting in a church where the Lord isn't present'.

Religion was present but He wasn't. What we tend to sometimes forget, is that the Religious Leaders of the day crucified Jesus. Jesus isn't interested in Religion. He's interested in Relationship.

*But you who are known as the Pharisees are rotten to the core! You've been poisoned by the nature of a venomous snake. How can your words be good and trustworthy if you are rotten within? For what has been stored up in your hearts will be heard in the overflow of your words!*

Matthews 12:34 TPT

*And you did not receive the 'spirit of religious duty,' leading you back into the fear of never being good enough. But you have received the 'Spirit of full acceptance,' enfolding you into the family of God.*

Romans 8:15 TPT

I got home that night and asked the Lord to send me to the right church where His Spirit is welcome and present. A couple of weeks later I walked into that church and was overjoyed to feel and experience His presence in a local church again.

It was within that first month that I went to my pastor and told him that I wanted to be baptised in the Holy Spirit. He was very excited about it and said they'd do it the following Saturday afternoon and would see if any of the other members wanted to be baptised as well.

I remember how excited I was on the day. I desperately wanted to walk in the full power of the Holy Spirit, to be able to pray in the Spirit and not waste any time in getting to where the Lord wanted to take me in my life.

It was such a big life-changing moment being baptised in the Holy Spirit in water and becoming a completely New creation in Christ.

Everything felt new and it was....

*My old identity has been co-crucified with Messiah and no longer lives; for the nails of His cross crucified me with Him. And now the essence of this new life is no longer mine, for the Anointed One lives His life through me. We live in union as one!*

Gal 2:20 TPT

*After the disciples' conversion experience they waited in Jerusalem as Jesus had instructed. They were ALL baptised in the Holy Spirit and spoke in tongues. Peter was no longer 'hiding away in fear' but now he was bold as he addressed the crowd.*

Acts 2:1 TPT

Because I had grown up with such a strong belief system that went completely against speaking in tongues, it didn't start straight away but I kept believing and a couple of months later the Lord woke me up in the middle of the night and gave me my first word. I was so excited and shortly after that I started to fluently pray in the Spirit.

This was something that I couldn't share with my parents or family at the time due to their strong beliefs against it. But what they all started noticing from then on, was how the fruit of the Holy Spirit started to manifest in my life as well as the gift of healing.

*But the fruit produced by the Holy Spirit within you is Devine love in all its varied expressions: joy that overflows, peace that subdues, patience that endures, kindness in action, a life full of virtue, faith that prevails, gentleness of heart and strength of spirit.*

Gal 5:22 TPT

*Those who are motivated by the flesh only pursue what benefits themselves. But those who live by the impulses of the Holy Spirit are motivated to pursue spiritual realities. For the mind-set of the flesh is death but the mind-set controlled by the Holy Spirit finds life and peace.*

Romans 8:5–6 TPT

# Chapter 8

# A year of being in the Secret Place

Life was just wonderful. My darlings Simba and Gracy were both doing so well, bringing me so much joy and love daily. My heart was burning with a desire and hunger for more of God and I was growing in my faith. My life felt full of love and blessings and my heart was filled with gratitude.

It was beginning of 2020 and I was super excited about the new year ahead. Every prophetic word that I'd received I'd kept very close to my heart believing and knowing it was going to come to pass. I had a constant expectancy growing inside my spirit, knowing my future was bright. Although I was still single, all my trust was in the Lord and He gave me so much peace and reassurance to just trust Him and know that He would bring my husband to me at the right time, in His divine timing.

The Holy Spirit prompted me from beginning of January to 'up' my daily health routine. He told me to start drinking coconut water daily and to add wheatgrass to my daily smoothies with my daily vitamins.

It was only 3 months later that I realised why He had prompted me to do that...

The weeks flew by and before I knew it, it was end of March and all of a sudden there was talk about a pandemic, a global pandemic... I remember when the first UK lockdown started – all of a sudden it really was just me, the Lord, Simba and Gracy every day.

The Holy Spirit directed me very clearly to stop watching television at that time. I've learned to never ask questions when the Holy Spirit asks me to do anything. For me obedience to Him is key in my life. So without hesitating I packed my television away and put it in my spare room and didn't think twice about it.

To be honest I didn't miss it at all. And looking back I'm so grateful that the Lord asked me to stop watching the news and television. People were stuck at home and through the media and television the enemy brought fear, anxiety and depression to people during that year.

*For God will never give you a spirit of fear but the Holy Spirit who gives you mighty power, love and self-control.*

2 Timothy 1:7 TPT

It was summer in the UK and we had one of the best summers ever weather wise. It was a long summer with long sunny days and I could spend all my time outside in my garden with Simba, Gracy and the Lord.

With all the time I had on my hands I started to watch daily teachings of Kevin Zadai and all of the Generals in the Kingdom. I wanted to learn as much as I could in the time I had from the top leaders in the Kingdom. I found myself spending 2–3 hours a day listening to these leaders preaching the gospel, speaking from the Spirit. The hunger grew more inside of me as I spent more time in the Word, learning and being transformed by the renewing of my mind.

*Do not be conformed to the pattern of this world but be transformed by the renewing of your mind.*

Rom 12:2 TPT

*Now it's time to be made new by every revelation that's been given to you. And to be transformed as you embrace the glorious Christ – within as your new life and live in union with Him!*

Ephesians 4:23 TPT

The Holy Spirit told me to start praying in tongues daily and to do it for at least 1–2 hours a day. There was no reason for me not to do it, because I had all the time. So I started first just praying for 30 minutes and then, like growing a muscle, it just started getting easier and easier. Before I knew it, I was praying sometimes for up to 3 hours at a time in my heavenly prayer language.

*And in a similar way, The Holy Spirit takes hold of us in our human frailty to empower us in our weakness, For example, at times we don't even know how to pray or know the best things to ask for. But the Holy Spirit rises up within us to super-intercede on our behalf, pleading to God with emotional sighs, too deep for words.*

*God, the searcher of our heart, knows fully our longings, yet He also understands the desires of the Spirit, because the Holy Spirit passionately pleads before God for us, his holy ones in perfect harmony with God's plan and our destiny.*

Rom 8:26–27 TPT

# Chapter 9

# A holiday marked by the Holy Spirit

It was in September of that year that I went back to Skiathos again for a holiday. I was so excited to go to my special island again, especially after all the lockdowns we had gone through. I was just about to leave church on the Sunday evening, when I got a message on my phone to say that my flight to Skiathos for the next day had been cancelled…

Immediately I felt the Spiritual Warfare and my heart tightened. I got home as quickly as possible to try and book another flight. I asked the Lord to please make a way and give me a flight. A short while later I found another flight and relief came over me. I had to pay for a new flight, which was not ideal but later I realised why the enemy was trying to stop me from going to Skiathos… little did I know what the Lord had in store for me when I got there…

I stayed in a beautiful area called Troulos in a self-catering apartment on a hill with the most beautiful view over the bay. The apartments belong to a lovely Greek couple with whom I'd become friends. It was so wonderful to enjoy the peace, sunshine, lovely food and rest in Skiathos again.

It was a Sunday morning and I went off to the local beach for a couple of hours before rushing back to my apartment to listen to the live streaming of my church service.

As I got to my apartment the lady was just finishing cleaning my room and asked why I was back so soon. I told her I didn't want to miss my church sermon online and it was just about to start. I'm pretty sure it wasn't something she'd heard very often from a guest on a Sunday morning.

I started watching the sermon online and as usual the presence of the Holy Spirit was very strong and it filled the room. As I lifted my hands to the Lord in worship, the Holy tears were streaming in His presence. There's no distance in the Spirit, which meant I felt the same presence of the Lord as they did back in the UK.

Just after finishing watching the sermon, I was filled to overflow with the Holy Spirit. I walked out of my apartment and bumped into the lady again. She asked me how the church service was and I told her how wonderful it had been and all the miracles that we'd seen the Lord doing there. And as I shared it all with her, the Holy Spirit prompted me to ask her if she had any pain in her body and to my surprise she said 'yes'. She said she had a lot of pain in her foot and also in her back. I asked her if I could pray with her for healing and immediately she said, 'yes please.'

We went into my room and as we walked in, she could immediately feel the thick presence of the Holy Spirit still in the room. All the hairs on her arm started standing up and I told her it was the presence of the Lord. I could feel this lady's deep strong faith and as I laid my hands on her back and prayed, the Holy Spirit came in power and healed her instantly and her pain was gone. She was so amazed, she started moving around and kept saying 'the pain is gone'.

Immediately she asked me to pray for her foot as well. Her foot was very swollen and she struggled to get her shoe off. I felt the Lord's heart and compassion for this beautiful lady. As I laid my hands on her foot and prayed for restoration, all pain left her immediately. Praise the Lord!

We were both standing there in awe of what the Holy Spirit was doing in front of our eyes. And just at that moment I asked her if she would like to give her heart to the Lord and without hesitation, she agreed... There, in my room in Skiathos, I had the honour of leading this precious lady into the Kingdom of God. I was filled with so much joy.

And without hesitating, she then told me about her children. She had triplets, two teenage boys and a girl. Her daughter had been struggling with severe depression and was not eating much at all. She asked me if I could please pray for her as well.

This mother's faith was stirred up and the Lord says in his Word, we only need faith the size of a mustard seed for a mountain to be moved and she had it. In front of me was a mother desperate for her child.

*Go! It shall be done for you as you have believed.*
*And his servant was healed at that moment.*

Matthew 8:13 TPT

That afternoon, around 15:00, she brought her daughter to my room. In she came, this very skinny shadow of a teenage girl. I couldn't help to notice there was no life in her eyes. She looked empty. She looked dead on the inside and my heart went out to her. I could feel the compassion welling up in me. I could tell she was only there because her mum asked her to come but she really didn't want to be there.

I also have to be very honest. In that moment I was a bit worried that she might start to manifest while I was praying for her but the Holy Spirit did a complete work in her and there was no manifestation of demons.

I laid my hands one above her chest and one on her back and commanded the depression to leave in Jesus Name. As I prayed, I felt something leave immediately and she felt it too. There was a real shift in the atmosphere and the Holy Spirit did it in an instant.

As the girl was standing in front of me, clearly amazed at what just happened, I asked her if I could lead her in a prayer to accept Jesus as her Lord and Saviour and she said 'yes'. Praise the Lord. After she accepted the Lord,

I could immediately see a change in her face. She stayed a little while and then said she was going back to their house downstairs.

It was only a minute later, while the mum was still busy talking to me, that we heard a sudden noise outside. We both ran out and saw the girl lying on the concrete outside their front door. We were both shocked and the mum said 'Oh no not again!' We immediately ran to her daughter. She seemed to have passed out and by the Lord's grace her head had missed the concrete. Her dad and brothers came running outside and we all picked her up and helped her inside into her room.

I sat next to her with my hand on her back and started praying in tongues. I was so confused and asked the Holy Spirit 'What on earth had just happened?' She had just given her life to the Lord and then she passed out and fell.

*But when the truth – giving Spirit comes, He will unveil the reality of every truth within you. He won't speak on His own but only what He hears from the Father and He will reveal to you Prophetically what is to come.*

John 16:13 TPT

*We do not know what we ought to pray for but the Spirit himself intercedes for us through wordless groans.*

Rom 8:26 NIV

It was probably after 5–10 minutes of praying in tongues, that the girl suddenly opened up and started telling me the truth and I was just in awe of how the Lord revealed the truth to me in that moment.

So she told me about the bullying at school.... and how long it had been going on and that that was the reason she had stopped eating and lost so much weight. That was the reason she had started to faint so much, because her body was too weak. My eyes welled up with tears as I listened to her talk about what she'd been going through and for how long it had been going on. And just there and then, through the Holy Spirit revealing the truth, I knew exactly what to pray for to break the attack of the bullying and commanded her appetite to come back in Jesus' name. I also felt led by the Holy Spirit to ask the mum for some olive oil. I prayed over the oil and used it to anoint the mum and daughter and also the girl's bedroom. I left there probably an hour later. I walked away again feeling like I'd just watched a movie. My heart was overflowing and all I could do was praise the Lord. All glory to Jesus.

What an incredible afternoon I had of being able to witness what the Lord did and how He transformed and healed both the mum and daughter and how they then both came into the Kingdom of Jesus.

I could feel in my Spirit Heaven's excitement and how they are all rejoicing about what just happened.

That night I went to bed and was just thanking the Lord for what He did for this family and that I'd had the privilege to witness it. My faith felt like it was going through the roof and I felt such a great excitement stirring up in my spirit for what was lying ahead in the future and God's plans for my life.

But the Holy Spirit wasn't done yet. Two days later the family invited me over for the afternoon. As soon as I walked in and saw the daughter, I was just blown away by what I saw.

The best way to describe it, is that if I had taken a picture of that girl three days before and a picture then, it would have looked like two completely different people. There she was, full of life, vibrancy, energy and her face was glowing, whereas before she looked like she was completely dead and empty on the inside. All Glory to God for the complete freedom and transformation He brought to this beautiful girl.

As I sat down with the dad and two brothers, they were so amazed about the transformation they had witnessed in their sister and daughter, that they all agreed for me to also lead them to give their lives to the Lord. It was such a beautiful moment. Afterwards the Lord led me to pray for the whole family while we held hands in a circle and as I prayed the thick strong presence of the Lord filled the atmosphere in that room and it was so beautiful.

I left their house with a heart overflowing with gratitude and in complete awe of what the Lord did.

He only needs our 'Yes' to be His vessel and He will do the rest.

I came back to the UK filled with so much excitement in my spirit of what the Lord had in store for me. I couldn't wait for Him to use me again.

But clearly the enemy was not very happy about what had happened in Skiathos and as soon as I got back, all hell broke loose and I knew exactly why my flight was all of a sudden cancelled the evening before I was supposed to fly from the UK to Skiathos.

Within 24 hours of my return to the UK my mum had a bad fall in her house and broke her leg. She had to be rushed to hospital and was tested for the Covid virus on arrival. She tested positive, although she was asymptomatic, which meant she was then placed in the Covid ward with all the other patients. Worry and fear overwhelmed me all at once.

At the same time within a week, Gracy's brand new outdoor cage had been completely destroyed. I walked outside to find it looking as if a bomb had exploded on top of it. It turned out that the water covering on the roof collected too much water and because it wasn't designed properly, the weight of the water destroyed the whole structure of it. I stood there looking at it, simply not being able to believe what had just happened, but I knew this was the enemy. He was clearly not happy. Just to top it off, money was then stolen from me through fraud as well.

This attack by the enemy pushed me into wanting to learn more about Spiritual Warfare and my true identity in Christ. To truly know the keys of how to resist the devil and fight back.

*So then, surrender to God. Stand up to the devil and resist him and he will flee in agony. Move your heart closer and closer to God and He will come even closer to you. But make sure you cleanse your life, you sinners and keep your heart pure and stop doubting.*

James 4:7–8 TPT

*The Lord will cause the enemies who rise up against you to be defeated before you; they will come out against you one way but flee before you seven ways.*

Deuteronomy 28:7 AMP

The next 5 months were quite challenging but the Lord strengthened me and I just kept pressing in deeper and deeper into Him and His promises. The UK went into yet another lockdown and I spent the cold winter by myself, with only the Lord, Simba and my dear Gracy.

I spent as much time as possible in the Word and online teachings. Listening and learning from the Generals in the Kingdom and growing stronger in my faith daily. Evenings were spent downstairs with Gracy and Simba while I worshipped for hours at a time in the sweet presence of the Holy Spirit.

There was a lot of challenges for my family in South Africa at the time and it felt as if the pressure became more and more intense by the day. I spent hours daily with them on video calls trying to support and comfort them where I could.

It was a lonely Christmas on my own with Simba and Gracy but the Lord was so faithful. It ended up being one of my best Christmases ever. The Lord's presence was so strong in my house and I had so much peace on the inside being excited about the new year and what the Lord had in store for me.

*I leave the gift of peace with you – My peace. Not the kind of fragile peace given by the world but my perfect peace.*

John 14:27 TPT

# Chapter 10

# A new gift

In February I started looking for a new job as finances had started to become very tight after not working for almost a year (due to the pandemic) and it seemed that it was a good time to get back into Dental Hygiene.

I hadn't been searching for a job for very long when the Lord highlighted a dental practice about 10–15 min drive from my house. I decided to go there as I saw that they were looking for a dental hygienist.

As I walked in, the receptionist sent me to the Practice Manageress' office and I immediately felt a sense of peace – like I was in the right place at exactly the right time. As I sat talking to the lovely practice manageress, I could feel the favour of the Lord on me and I knew that this was a gift from Him. Everything went well and it seemed like they were happy to arrange a formal interview with the principle of the practice so he could meet me.

As I left there, the sense of relief and peace was overwhelming. I knew in my heart, that this was my new practice where I would work and that it was purely the Lord's Favour that had brought this job to me as a gift. My heart overflowed with gratitude. I never thought I would get a job so close to home.

There's just no end to His love and faithfulness.

It was also during this time that the Lord started to give me multiple dreams. He was speaking to me very clearly about the new year and He was very clear on taking me into something new. He wanted new levels of intimacy with me and for me to step into that, He told me that my season at the church where I was, had ended and that it was time for me to leave.

It took a good couple of months to finally tell the pastor and his wife that the Lord had spoken to me and told me that my season with them had ended. I wanted to make 100% sure it was what God wanted but God kept confirming it over and over again – showing me that if I didn't leave, He couldn't take me into this new season of my life.

This was, I believe, a big test of my obedience to the Lord. At that moment, the pastor's wife and I were very close and we were best friends. It wasn't easy for me to take this step of obedience but the Lord is so good, so kind and so faithful.

On the day I shared the news with them that I was leaving, the Lord gave me a final and probably the best confirmation of all through something the pastor's wife said to me. Immediately, as soon as I stepped into His obedience, an overwhelming sense of peace flooded my heart and I was super excited about my new season with the Lord and where He was taking me.

I blessed the pastor and his wife and never looked back as I moved forward with the Lord into His grace and His plans for my life.

I was excited about my new job but the enemy was definitely not overly happy about it. I felt quite intense warfare as I could sense he didn't want me to have it.

There was quite a lot of delay before I could start. The management took almost 3 weeks to give notice to the current hygienist to leave and she wanted 3 months before leaving. This meant I had to find locum work to cover myself financially until I started.

At the time there wasn't a lot of locum work available and I ended up having to drive 1.5 hours one way to one job where I was being paid at a very low rate. It felt like the pressure was building up and after long days of spending at least 3 hours on the road and having to phone family members in the evening to support them emotionally, I knew I wouldn't be able to continue like that for much longer.

I remember coming home one day, sitting in my car on my driveway and talking to my dad on the phone, who was going through a very difficult time and needed my support. I remember feeling emotionally so tired and drained, that I just bursted into tears. I couldn't be strong for everyone else anymore when I felt like it was all just becoming too much to handle.

My poor dad was so shocked, he asked me straight away why I was crying and I couldn't even tell him.

I just said, 'I don't know Dad.' As I sat there and looked out of my car window there on my side mirror was a Robin that looked straight at me...

This is something that had never happened before and it was so significant to me in that moment, because the Lord often shows His presence to me by showing me a Robin. This made me cry even more. The Lord was telling me 'My daughter, I'm right here by your side. I'm with you. Trust me. I've got this.'

And then, all of a sudden unexpectedly Jesus destroyed the delay in an instant! I got a phone call from the new practice a day later asking me whether there was any chance I could start the very next day....

I was completely in awe and wasn't expecting it as it was still another 2 months at least until the current hygienist was supposed to leave. It turned out she was about to ask the principle that very day if she could stay another 6 months but 'something' happened and she was immediately fired that day.

I knew this was the Lord's Devine intervention – Him coming in power destroying all delay from the enemy to block this new gift that He had for me.

The enemies that were trying to stop and delay my gift, were now fleeing in seven directions from me.

The sense of relief that I instantly felt, was immense. I felt like I could breathe properly again. Like a very heavy weight was lifted off from me. And 2 days later I started my new job...

*No weapon formed against you shall succeed.*

Isaiah 54:17 TPT

*When we live our lives within the shadow of God Most High, our secret hiding place, we will always be shielded from harm. How then could evil prevail against us or disease infect us?*

Psalms 91: 9–11 TPT

*For here is what the Lord has spoken to me: 'Because you have delighted in me as my great lover, I will greatly protect you.*

*I will set you in a high place, safe and secure before My face.*

*I will answer your cry for help every time you pray,*

*and you will find and feel My presence even in your time of pressure and trouble.*

*I will be your glorious hero and give you a feast.'*

Psalm 91:14–15 TPT

The first 3 months at my new job was quite intense, trying to get back into the rhythm of work. The Lord started to stretch me a bit slowly but surely out of my old comfort zone into the 'new' that He had for me so that I could receive everything He wanted to give to me through this job.

After settling in, I kept looking back, knowing it was His grace that got me through that first 6 months of probation. The team I worked with were all so lovely and I left work every day thanking the Lord for this wonderful gift. Only 10–15 min drive from home; I simply couldn't have asked for a better job, a better team or a better location.

*If you, imperfect as you are, know how to lovingly take care of your children and give them what's best, how much more ready is your Heavenly Father to give wonderful gifts to those who ask Him?*

Matthew 7:11 TPT

# Chapter 11

# Faith that moves mountains

I used to go to South Africa at least once to twice a year to see my family but due to the pandemic, this wasn't possible for 2 years. It was the longest time without seeing them and I couldn't wait for South Africa to come off the red list of countries to visit after the pandemic.

As soon as South Africa came off the red list in October, I booked my ticket to go there for 3 weeks in December. I started packing immediately. Three weeks before leaving, my suitcase was packed and I was ready to go and was beyond excited. I couldn't get there quickly enough. My whole family had been through a very challenging, difficult time and I just wanted to be with them more than ever. My suitcase was packed with gifts for everyone and I literally had to sit on my suitcase to be able to close it properly.

It was 3 days before flying out that I saw the news – South Africa was back on the red list…..

I went to work the next day and the practice manageress came to see me before I started work, to see if I was ok after the news. As soon as I saw her, I asked her to please not talk about it, because I needed to somehow get through that day full of patients miraculously and if I dared to think about the possibility of not being able to see my family, I would just start crying.

I went straight to the Lord and the Lord said to me 'Lida, you need to trust me. I want you to still get on your flight, no matter what the situation looks like in the natural. Don't fear and don't doubt, just trust me my daughter'.

> *Now you are ready, my bride, to come with me as we climb the highest peaks together. Come with me through the archway of trust.*
>
> *We will look down from the crest of the glistening mounts and from the summit of our sublime sanctuary. Together we will wage war in the lion's den and the leopard's lair as they watch nightly for their prey.*

Song of Songs 4:8 TPT

I remember lying in bed that night, saying to the Lord, Lord I don't care how you get me there, if it means to transport/translate my spirit, please just take my suitcase as well so that I have my clothes with me. I'm sure He must've thought it was a bit funny that I was thinking about my suitcase. . . My faith was raised to new heights because I knew somehow the Lord would make it happen. He would make a way when it looked like there was no way at all. With God nothing is impossible.

All my friends that had flights booked to go to South Africa cancelled them immediately but I didn't...

I went to the airport that day and I could feel the intense warfare of the enemy to try and keep me from going. I'd never felt like that before flying to South Africa but the level of uncertainty and tension was unexpected and very high.

I was convinced I would be on an empty plane that day but to my surprise my flight was completely fully booked. It seemed like I wasn't the only one that was going to go no matter what.

I arrived at my parents' house safely and was quite shocked when I saw them. I could immediately see that the time apart had taken its toll on them. I was just overjoyed to finally be with them and determined to make the most of every precious moment together.

It was my third day there and we were busy with a barbeque when I saw the news. I will never forget that moment. It felt like my Spirit leaped with joy out of my body. South Africa had just been removed from the red list!!! My faith jumped through the roof! Jesus, you did it! You did it! Just like You said You would. All Glory to God.

I spent 3 weeks with my mum and dad. We were super careful not to go to restaurants, coffee shops or public places like we used to do. It was only for the food shop that I had to go into the shops but I made sure we all sanitised all the time. We spent Christmas together. It was so special and I couldn't take enough photos and videos to capture the wonderful moments together.

But I couldn't help thinking in the back of my mind *would this be the last Christmas together? How long until I would be able to see them again?* I left those questions with the Lord and knew every moment was a gift to appreciate and to not think any further or allow the enemy to steal our joy and time together.

It was just after Christmas that I felt like I was getting a bit of sinusitis. That's something that I'd had a couple of times over the years before when coming to South Africa, so I didn't think anything of it. My time with my parents were running out and a couple of days later I had to leave for Cape Town to quickly see my brother, niece and sister-in-law, before flying back to the UK.

I arranged for a shuttle service to pick me up. It was with a very heavy heart that I got in the car after saying good bye to my elderly parents, but the moment I got in the car, I felt the presence of the Lord with the driver and we immediately started talking and sharing about our faith and walk with the Lord. And all of a sudden I no longer had a heavy heart.

I was so excited, because I love how God always divinely choose who to place next to me and I always sense that He had it all planned out to be that way. Either I had to give a message to the person or the Lord would give me a message through the other person. Either way, it's always a blessing.

At exactly 13:00 the driver pulled the car over to the side of the road and said he had been doing the same thing for the last year and always prayed Psalm 91 at 13:00 no matter where he was. So we both prayed it together and on we went to Cape Town.

When I got to my brothers' place, I had to quickly go for my Covid test to have my results in time before flying back to the UK 2 days later. Later that evening, I was having dinner with my brother when he told me the very unexpected news 'Lida your test results have just come through on my phone. You tested positive'.

At first I thought he was making a joke – surely not! I was feeling 100%. How can this be? To my surprise I saw it was true and my heart sank. Immediately I was gripped with uncertainty and fear.

But the Holy Spirit kept whispering to me 'read Psalm 91 and meditate on it. I'm with you, my daughter, do not fear.'

So that's what I did. All along the Lord was actually planning to bless me through this extra week I had to stay in South Africa, I just didn't know it at that moment.

I didn't actually realise how emotionally exhausted I was after the 3 weeks I'd spent with my mum and dad, helping them and supporting them. They both had their own difficult issues and I guess trying to help them and be there for them, made me feel like I was carrying their loads as well.

So all of a sudden, I had to isolate at my brother's house and could sleep and rest every day. I felt like I could sleep for days non-stop, so I slept as much as I could and even enjoyed a bit of sunshine in their back garden, which was a big blessing after the cold, windy days I had at my parents' the whole of December.

After 3 days, we tested again and my test came back negative. It was such great news, because it meant my sister-in-law and my precious little niece could join us at the house. They had been staying with my sister-in-law's mum until it was safe to come back.

Initially I would've only had a day with my precious little niece but now I had 3 full days to spend with her, my brother and sister-in-law. For those of you who don't have your own children, know how extra precious it is to have a niece or nephew. They feel like your own children. After not seeing my little niece for 2 years she had grown so much. We had such a special time together and I'm so grateful to God for these extra 'Grace days' that He made possible for me through having to stay an extra week.

As I was sitting on the plane on my way back to the UK, I watched the most beautiful sunrise and the whole sky turned orange. It was so beautiful. As I was sitting there, I could feel all the worry rising up in me about my family and again I heard the Lord's voice 'Just trust me my daughter. Trust me that I will take care of your family in South Africa. Do not fear or worry'. And as I heard his voice, I fell into a deep peaceful sleep, knowing He had my back.

*'Surrender your anxiety. Be still and realize that I am God. I am God above all the nations, and I am exalted throughout the whole earth.'*

Psalms 46:10 TPT

I got back to the UK with my faith being on a whole new level after the last month's journey with the Lord. He is so faithful. He supernaturally provided financially for me for the extra week I couldn't work in the UK. And as I looked back, it was all so clear to me. Testing positive was a 'blessing in disguise' that I hadn't seen at that very moment.

I had missed my dear Simba and Gracy so much, I couldn't wait to see their beautiful furry faces. They were so cute and so happy to see me. Their little faces were smiling from ear to ear. And my evenings were back to blissful times of worship surrounded by the presence of the Lord, Simba and Gracy.

The weeks went by so quickly as I got back into the rhythm of work again. Before we knew it, the first daffodils started to pop up in the garden. I always fill up with so much excitement as the first signs of spring appear after the long, cold UK winters. Slowly the days were getting longer and all the beautiful flowers had started to come up. Everything was coming back to life.

# Chapter 12

# A new season is coming

2022 started to feel a bit like life was 'back to normal' again after the pandemic. People were travelling all over the world and were excited about their holidays booked in advance.

Gracy was now 5 years old and still every time I looked at her or spent time with her, she made my heart melt. She always made me laugh and it was as if she knew

exactly how to do it. Every time I looked at her, I knew in my heart what a precious gift she was and that every day with her was a gift.

The Holy Spirit showed me how to rebuild her outdoor cage after it was destroyed by the force of the water. I remember sitting outside, just looking at it, wondering how on earth I was going to get rid of the cage and replace it. The metal was bent at all different angles. I just sat there and stared at it, asking the Lord what to do. I couldn't afford to buy another cage like that or get someone to build it. While all the questions went through my head, in a very gentle and still voice the Holy Spirit started to whisper instructions in my ear step by step on what to do. He led me to dismantle the cage and rebuild it in a way that was even better than before. Only the Lord could do that. I was amazed and so excited for Gracy to see her new cage.

July was filled with lovely warm days in the UK and my days off and spare time was spent outside with Gracy and Simba. In the evenings I spent all my time, worshipping, online studying and listening and learning from the Generals in the Kingdom. Simba would be sleeping blissfully while Gracy darling was hopping all around me asking for cuddles and strokes. It was my 'happy place'. Worshipping the Lord while my two fur babies were right next to me.

It was beginning of August when I went for a lovely walk in the forest one morning. It was a beautiful sunny morning and as I was walking, I heard the Lord say to me 'You are stepping into a new season of your life, my daughter...'

I was so excited when I heard the Lord's voice speak straight into my heart as I was more than ready for a new season. I was super excited about what the Lord had in store for me in this new season but little did I know what I was about to experience…

Nothing could've prepared me for it and I was most certainly not expecting it.

It was towards the end of August when I got some kind of virus that went straight into my chest and made me cough a lot. It was just as I was starting to feel better, that one evening I noticed that something wasn't quite right with Gracy. She was not moving as much as usual and when I stroked her, it looked as if she might've lost a bit of weight. She'd been eating the same amount of food as usual but she definitely looked like she lost a bit of weight.

The next day I drove home in my lunch hour to go and check on her. As soon as I saw her, I knew I had to take her straight to the vets. I could just see it in her eyes. Luckily the vets were just around the corner, so I took her straight there and by the grace of God, they could see her quickly. My heart felt tight. Gracy had never been ill or unwell in the 5.5 years that she'd been with me. She'd always been super healthy.

The vet looked up at me after examining her. She had a worrying look on her face and said 'It's serious. She's got a chest infection that's already deep in her chest'. My heart sank and the tears started to well up in my eyes.

She said that Gracy would have to come back daily for the next 7 days to be injected with antibiotics. I knew that wasn't possible so I explained to the vet that it would be too stressful for Gracy if I had to take her in every day for 7 days to get injected and asked the vet if there was any chance I could give her the injections myself. To this day I'm still surprised that she actually agreed but I think she could see the tears and desperation in my eyes. It was the Lord's grace. So she injected Gracy and told me to come in the next day to collect the syringes that she would get ready for me.

I quickly took Gracy home and had to rush back to work. All the way back I was thanking the Lord that He prompt me to go home in my lunch hour to check on her and my heart filled up with faith. The Lord's got this. Gracy will be ok....

The next day I got the syringes and started to inject Gracy daily. I didn't enjoy having to do it but I knew there was no other way. I was worried that it might be hurting her but I kept telling her that she needed her medication to get better. Over the next two days I started to see a wonderful improvement in her. Gracy started to get her energy back and I could see her cute funny personality coming back again. A huge sense of relief came over me and I was praising the Lord and rejoicing. My Gracy was going to be ok. 'Thank you Jesus, Thank you Jesus, Thank you Jesus.' I felt such a huge relief, everything was going to be ok. That was Saturday...

By Tuesday I saw Gracy taking a turn that I wasn't expecting... she started to decline. All of a sudden fear started coming in as I started to see what I had been expecting the least. I rushed back to the vets for more antibiotics.

I cried out to the Lord, 'Please Lord, save my Gracy. You have done it before. Please do it again'. I prayed over her, laying hands over and over and I kept believing. 'The Lord will come through and He will save her just like He did before.'

By Wednesday I couldn't go to work as I was too emotional and wanted to be with her and check on her. By the grace of God the practice manageress understood that I was going through a very tough emotional time and couldn't focus or work.

By Thursday I could see there was still no improvement but I still kept fighting for her, praying and praying and praying. I couldn't eat or sleep. It all felt like a horrible nightmare and I just wanted to wake up and see that it wasn't true. My heart was breaking into pieces every time I looked at her. This was my baby girl, my Gracy, my precious little girl whom I loved more than words could ever describe. Only the Lord knew how much love was in my heart for her.

I kept pleading with the Lord 'Please Lord, you can still save her if You want to.'

It was Friday evening and as I looked at her, I knew I would have to take her to the vets the next morning unless she improved – for which I still had a little bit of hope.

I woke up the next morning walking to her room with a very heavy heart and as soon as I saw her, I knew, it was time to set her free. I phoned the vets and told them

I would be there in 5 minutes. I thank the Lord that it was only around the corner from me. I sobbed my heart out and I sat with her stroking her and telling her that today was going to be her best day ever. That in the next 20 minutes she was going to go straight to heaven and she would be free forever. Free to live the best life ever and run around as much as she wanted to and that she would be so happy, healthy and free.

It was only God's grace that gave me the strength to quickly go to the vets. I still remember driving with her to the vets and saying to her through my tears 'Gracy run fast and jump high for mummy in heaven'.

The vet that usually saw Gracy wasn't in that day, so when the vet came out to me, I told her Gracy was wild and because of that, it wasn't as straight forward as just injecting her. They had to first put her to sleep in a container with sleeping gas before injecting her so she could pass over to heaven.

I wasn't allowed to go with her. It all happened so quickly. When the vet was ready to take her in her carry container, I said one last goodbye and sobbed as I said 'My darling it's all going to be over now. I love you so much.' Then she took my Gracy away.

I waited outside in my car and cried my heart out but at the same time I felt a sense of relief knowing that Gracy wouldn't suffer a minute longer.

It was about 10 minutes later that the vet came outside with Gracy's little body in her carry container. She gave her to me and said Gracy fell asleep and they then gave her the injection after she had already fallen asleep. This gave me so much peace knowing that she literally went to sleep and woke up in heaven. She didn't have to go through the stress of someone holding her and giving her the final injection. Even at the end the Lord poured His grace out.

I got back in my car and looked at her pink container. I just sobbed and sobbed. It felt like my heart was in a million pieces. I had never expected this. I knew that I would have to give her back to the Lord one day but I never expected it to be then. She had been so healthy and within 10 days she'd died.

I went home and went straight to her room. I opened her container and there she was, my beautiful baby girl. I laid my hands on her beautiful body and started stroking her, crying my heart out. Her little body was still warm. How long I sat there for I don't know but I just sat there with her, holding her, stroking her, crying and telling her how much I love her.

It felt like my whole world had come crashing down in a minute…. For 5.5 years she had been such a big part of my life. The Lord brought her to me at the most painful difficult time of my life when I needed her the most. No words could describe what a great blessing and gift from the Lord she had been.

It was 24 hours later that I felt ready to lay her little body to rest. I wasn't really prepared for the question when the vet asked me if I wanted to keep her body but without hesitating I immediately said 'yes'.

I sat outside in my beautiful garden on the bench under the trees with her on my lap and cried, saying the last goodbye. It was then that Simba came over to me. At this point he hadn't realised that Gracy had gone to heaven, so he jumped up next to me on the bench to look at what was in Gracy's container. It was only then when he saw Gracy's little body, that he realised what had happened. I will never forget the shock on his little face as he saw that it was Gracy. His whole face changed and he looked distressed. He jumped off the bench and just walked away. I could see how sad and shocked he was. He loved Gracy and she had been a part of his life for 5.5 years. They had a very special bond and she was very fond of him.

I folded Gracy's little body in one of my t-shirts and then wrapped her in her beautiful blanket that used to be on her cage. I placed her little body into the small grave under the trees and placed my favourite beautiful painted metal heart on top and filled up her grave. I covered it with a concrete slab and placed the red metal heart that used to hang on her cage on top. I placed her favourite parsley plant next to it and a beautiful light blue cross next to it.

When I look back, I know the Lord held me so tightly in his arms and carried me through that time with His grace. I didn't want to let her go, and I certainly wasn't ready for it, but it was the Lord's time to call her home and I had to give her back to Him no matter how much it hurt.

It was a couple of days later while I was sitting on that bench in my garden under the trees, looking at Gracy's grave, when the Lord dropped a message in my spirit and said to me 'I want you to write a book "A Gift called Gracy". I heard it so clear in my spirit and in my heart but I left it in my heart until 6 months later when the Lord said it again to me in a dream. 'I want you to write this book.' That's when I realised, Gracy was not just a gift for me, she's going to be a gift for many as God continues to pour out His grace through this story.

It was a couple of days after Gracy had gone to heaven when a friend phoned me and gave me a prophetic message that the Lord had for me. This message from the Lord blessed me tremendously to accept what had just happened.

She phoned me and said that the Lord is taking me into a new season of my life and Gracy represented the previous season in my life that was now over. Gracy had to die and be buried as a prophetic sign that it's the end of the previous season and I'm stepping into the new season. I couldn't step into the new season with Gracy still being a part of it. I remembered how clearly the Lord told me, that morning in August walking in the forest, that I was stepping into a new season that He had for me. I just didn't know that I would have to let go of my little Gracy.

This gave me so much peace and also showed me that as much and as persistently as I had been praying for Gracy to be healed and fighting for her life through warfare to be saved, it would have never happened, no matter what, because it was God's appointed time to take her back to Him. She was a gift from Him and I always knew that every day with her was a beautiful 'grace gift' from my loving Heavenly Father that I would have to return one day.

Now I understood that it had to happen this way so that I could step into the new season that He had planned for me. It had to happen. I couldn't stop or prevent it.

*Every part of you is so beautiful, my darling.*
*Perfect is your beauty, without flaw within.*
*Now you are ready, my bride,*
*To come with Me as we climb the highest peaks*
*together.*

Song of Songs 4:7 TPT

About 6 months later I took Simba for his yearly vaccination at the vets. I was sitting in the waiting room and heard 'Simba Basson' being called out. I couldn't see the vet, just got up and walked towards the surgery and as I looked up, I saw her face. It was Gracy's vet and as she saw my face and realised it was me, she filled with excitement and said, 'Oh it's you! How's dear Gracy doing?'

It felt like the words hit me straight in my stomach. She didn't know – I was so hoping the other vet would've told her.

I had to hold the tears back as I told her the news that 'Gracy is now free and in heaven'.

As I walked outside, holding back the tears, I realised once again how special my dear Gracy was and always would be.

It was a couple of months later that I had a very clear Prophetic dream from the Lord about my life. I was sitting on an aeroplane with Gracy on my lap holding her in between my hands. I looked up for a second and when I looked down again, I was holding a dove in between my hands.

This dream was a wonderful confirmation from the Lord of my ministry and how it will be led by the Holy Spirit.

*All our direction and ministries will flow from Christ and lead us deeper into Him, the anointed Head of his body, the church.*

Eph 4:15 TPT

*Not by might, not by power, but by My Spirit.*

Zachariah 4:1 NIV

*For I know the plans I have for you, declares the Lord, plans to prosper you and not to harm you, plans to give you hope and a future.*

Jeremiah 29:11 NIV

She was not only a precious gift to me but she will also be to many who would read her story. A story that highlights God's wonderful and perfect grace that's freely available for all who choose Jesus as their Lord and Saviour.

If you have not yet received Jesus as your Lord and Saviour and you have felt His presence touching you while reading this book, then you have an opportunity to give your life to Him right now.

I will lead you in a very short prayer that will change your life forever...

If that is you, then just read these words right there where you are and open your heart.

*Lord Jesus today I choose to accept you as Lord and Saviour of my life.*
*Wash me clean with your blood now and forgive me for all my sins.*
*I receive your Holy Spirit right now Lord.*
*In Jesus' name.*

Amen

*Now if anyone is enfolded into Christ, he has become an entirely New person. All that is related to the old order has vanished. Behold everything is fresh and new.*

2 Corinthians 5:17 TPT

*You have all become true children of God by faith in Jesus the Anointed One! It was faith that immersed you into Jesus, the Anointed One and now you are covered and clothed with His Anointing.*

Gal 3:26 TPT

*Now we're no longer living like slaves under the law but we enjoy being God's very own sons and daughters. And because we're His, we can access everything our Father has – for we are heirs of God through Jesus, the Messiah!*

Gal 4:7 TPT

*...live your life empowered by God's free-flowing grace, which is your true strength, found in the anointing of Jesus and your Union with Him.*

2 Timothy 2:1 TPT

# Amazing Grace

*Amazing Grace how sweet the sound that saved a wretch like me!*

*I once was lost, but now I'm found, was blind, but now I see.*

*'Twas grace that taught my heart to fear, and grace my fears relieved; How precious did that Grace appeared the hour I first believed!*

*Through many dangers, toils and snares I have already come;*

*'tis grace has brought me safe thus far, and Grace will lead me home.*

*The Lord has promised good to me, his word my hope secures; he will my shield and portion be as long as life endures.*

*The earth shall soon dissolve like snow, the sun forbear to shine; but God who called me here below will be forever mine.*

*When we've been there ten thousand years,*
*Bright shining as the sun,*
*We've no less days to sing God's praise*
*Than when we'd first begun.*

Milton Keynes UK
Ingram Content Group UK Ltd.
UKHW020908300424
441987UK00014B/565

9 781803 817705